CRaZy EXTREME GUITAR TECHNIQUES

BY JOE BENNETT

WISE PUBLICATIONS
London / New York / Paris / Sydney / Copenhagen / Berlin / Madrid / Tokyo

Published by:
Wise Publications
8/9 Frith Street, London W1D 3JB, England.

Exclusive Distributors:
Music Sales Limited
Distribution Centre, Newmarket Road,
Bury St. Edmunds, Suffolk IP33 3YB England.
Music Sales Pty Limited
120 Rothschild Avenue, Rosebery, NSW 2018, Australia.
Music Sales Corporation
257 Park Avenue South, New York, NY10010, USA.

Order no. AM957814
ISBN: 0-7119-8224-4
This book © 2003 by Wise Publications.

Written by Joe Bennett.
Edited by Sorcha Armstrong.
Cover & book design by Fresh Lemon.
Music processed by Simon Troup.
Picture research by Dave Brolan & Sarah Bacon.

Artist photographs courtesy of London Features International,
except for Billy Sheehan (p58) - George Chin.
Photography by Darrin Jenkins.
Models: Matt Bragg, Enda Parker, Joe Bennett and Helen Sanderson.
Additional research by Jill Warren, Kit Morgan, Simon Troup and
Ross Bennett.

Printed in the United Kingdom.

Your Guarantee of Quality:
As publishers, we strive to produce every book to the highest
commercial standards. This book has been carefully designed to
minimise awkward page turns and to make playing from it a real
pleasure. Particular care has been given to specifying acid-free,
neutral-sized paper made from pulps which have not been
elemental chlorine bleached. This pulp is from farmed sustainable
forests and was produced with special regard for the environment.
Throughout, the printing and binding have been planned to ensure
a sturdy, attractive publication which should give years of enjoyment.
If your copy fails to meet our high standards, please inform us
and we will gladly replace it.

www.musicsales.com

INTRODUCTION

This is the most important guitar book you can buy. Some books might make you a better player, show you new chords, or help you to learn more about music theory. But only this one can show you the REALLY essential techniques...

Ever since **Aaron 'T-bone' Walker** played a guitar behind his head (whilst doing the splits – respect!) in the early 1940s, guitarists have tried to find new ways of playing their instrument. In the 1960s **Jimi Hendrix** famously plucked the strings with his teeth (or did he? see page 16) and even set his guitar alight. In the 1970s **Pete Townshend** plugged his guitar into early synthesisers. In the 1980s **Nils Lofgren** would take a solo while doing a back-flip on a trampoline. And in the 1990s US rock band **Mr Big** played their guitars with electric drills. Sadly, in recent years guitar players have tended to concentrate more on accurate musicianship and good guitar sounds.

With your help we can change things. Keep this book with you at all times. Whenever you play live, or even practise in front of friends, use as many of these ancient skills as you can. Abuse the instrument by hurling it around at previously untried angles. Find new tendon-challenging playing positions. Unearth hitherto undiscovered guitaristic uses for household objects. Remember, if you only ever use your guitar to make great music, these important disciplines could be lost to history forever.

The future is in your hands. Act now.

PREPOSTEROUS POSITIONS

There is one correct position to play the classical guitar – on your left knee, with a footstool under the left foot, and the neck at a 45 degree angle (see below). One day in the mid-18th century, a classical guitarist turned up for a gig without the footstool, and put the guitar on his right knee instead. From that day onward, people the world over realised that the guitar was easier to play in almost any other position than the left knee.

This led to the development of new ways of playing the guitar, and was directly responsible for the great European footstool industry collapse of 1784.

The legacy of these early right-knee pioneers still remains – there are still thousands of players striving to find new ways of avoiding correct classical technique. In this section, we discuss some of the greats – T-bone, Hendrix, Parfitt and Tufnel – and learn how, in a small way, our own guitar playing can benefit humbly from their revolutionary approaches.

Left: Correct classical position

Right: Incorrect classical position

Jimi, of course, is playing upside-down, back to front, on a right-handed guitar, played left handed, with the strings the other way, and his back turned towards the camera, with a reverse upstroke from the plectrum. It is rumoured that when this photo was taken he was playing the solo from 'All Along the Watchtower' backwards.

TECHNIQUE: *Behind the head*

AS USED BY: *Aaron 'T-bone Walker', Jimi Hendrix*

REQUIREMENTS: *Guitar, strap, head*

DIFFICULTY FACTOR: *2/10* **PREPOSTEROUSNESS RATING:** *8/10*

This is actually much easier than it looks. When you put the guitar behind your head, your picking and fretting hand are in the same position (relative to the guitar) as they would be when playing normally. As long as you can play without seeing where your hands are or moving position (suggest nice friendly minor pentatonic scale box shape) you can solo away to your heart's content until your audience or your shoulders tire. **HINT – the audience may become tired first.**

WARNING

MUCH EASIER ON A STRAT OR LES PAUL DUE TO BODY SHAPE. ALMOST IMPOSSIBLE TO ACHIEVE ON SOME DESIGNS OF EARLY 16TH CENTURY LUTE.

TECHNIQUE: *Lap position*

AS USED BY: *Lap steel & Hawaiian players, Jeff Healey*

REQUIREMENTS: *Guitar, lap, bottleneck & open tunings*

DIFFICULTY FACTOR: 5/10   **PREPOSTEROUSNESS RATING:** 9/10

This is very difficult to do while standing up, but with the right guitar (suggest f-hole semi-solid) and strap tension it can be achieved. It originated as the 'normal' technique for **Hawaiian guitarists**, and is still in use by all **lap steel players** today. Tune the guitar to an open chord (open G tuning – DGDGBD – is a good starting point) and use a bottleneck (also coffee cup, empty beer glass, cigarette lighter, kitchen knife etc.). Then play simple slide licks on one or two strings, employing the unused fingers of the picking hand to mute the remaining strings. **HINT – playing melodies on a single string looks more impressive than regular slide technique.**

If you are using the strap, make sure the guitar balances when it's in the flat position. If not, you will need to stand on one leg throughout the solo, propping the guitar up with your knee. The more experienced player may wish to take this opportunity to duck-walk (see page 50).

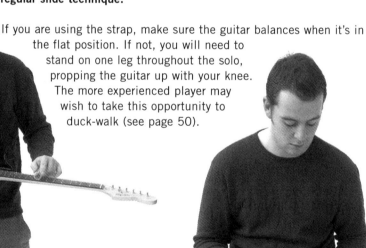

WARNING

IT'S ALMOST IMPOSSIBLE TO PLAY REGULAR NORMAL-TUNED BARRE CHORDS IN THIS POSITION.

The incredible Jeff Healey, playing in his customary lap position. Note the preposterous plectra on the guitar stand.

WARNING

CAN BE MISINTERPRETED
AS SLIGHTLY RUDE.

*Horseback
standard position*

*Horseback
comfort position with
reduced dignity option*

TECHNIQUE: *Horseback*

AS USED BY: *Prince*

REQUIREMENTS: *Electric guitar, long strap with strap-locks*

DIFFICULTY FACTOR: *9/10*   **PREPOSTEROUSNESS RATING:** *9/10*

Extend the guitar strap as far as it will go into the standard **Ramones** position (early period, strap length approx. 1.82m). Then push the whole body of the guitar behind you, lean forward and bring the headstock up between your legs. You should now have your picking hand behind you and your fretting hand in front. Play the guitar as normal (lead licks around the 5th-7th fret area are usually easiest).

ALTERNATIVELY – take the whole guitar off, leaving the strap attached, then step into the gap between strap and guitar. You should now have a leg either side of the guitar and the strap in the normal position. This position makes the guitar easier to play, but can be less dignified when returning to normal playing position.

Here, Edward Van Halen has foolishly attempted a combined machine-gun horseback 45 degree twist while standing on one leg and executing a whammy bar dive whilst gurning. Even the greats over-reach themselves sometimes.

TECHNIQUE: *Vertical hold*

AS USED BY: *Jimmy Page, Kiss, Status Quo, Slipknot*

REQUIREMENTS: *Electric guitar*

DIFFICULTY FACTOR: *2/10*   **PREPOSTEROUSNESS RATING:** *3/10*

The standard **Page** hold is pure showmanship and has very little benefit to the player (apart from looking cool, obviously). Pluck a fretted note and hold the entire guitar by its neck between your thumb and fretting finger. If you have very strong fingers it is possible to create vib by waving the guitar in mid air. A variation on this is to pluck the strings while supporting the body of the guitar on your thigh or pelvis – this frees up the fretting hand to play lead licks.

The **Parfitt** hold is unique to the man himself, but is in fact a very practical way of playing rhythm guitar. Simply hold the guitar on a strap as normal, but tilt it so that the headstock is closer to your head. The strumming hand is then at full stretch, so your rhythm playing needs to pivot from the shoulder and elbow rather than the wrist. The fretting hand is in the perfect position for chord playing.

Slipknot guitarists **Mick #7** and **James #4** have been known to use a Half-**Parfitt** vertical hold in the band's legendary stage shows. This may be mere coincidence, or a direct acknowledgement of **Status Quo**'s considerable influence on the band.

the Page hold

the Parfitt hold

WARNING

THE TWO TYPES OF VERTICAL HOLD ARE MUTUALLY EXCLUSIVE. DO NOT ATTEMPT TO PLAY PAGE LEAD GUITAR PHRASES WHILE HOLDING THE GUITAR IN THE PARFITT POSITION.

Standard vertical hold with forward crotch-thrust on a twin-neck. The thumb plays F at the first fret.

Basic machine-gun, ascending to semi-vertical hold.

Triple machine-gun hold with thigh support. Bassist Alan Lancaster is bravely attempting a conversion to a vertical hold but is struggling to reach.

TECHNIQUE: *Machine Gun*

AS USED BY: *Spinal Tap, Status Quo, Bruce Springsteen*

REQUIREMENTS: *Electric guitar, strap*

DIFFICULTY FACTOR: *2/10 (Basic)   5/10 (Advanced)*

PREPOSTEROUSNESS RATING: *3/10 (Basic)   8/10 (Advanced)*

Hold the guitar out horizontally, with the headstock facing the audience. Stretch the fretting hand out as far away from the body as you can. A basic Machine Gun can be attempted using regular barre chords (e.g. 5th fret) but the headstock protrudes at a disappointing un-intimidating angle. It's usually better to play lead licks at the 12th or even 17th fret, allowing for a 'bullet sweep' from left to right and back again.

In the earliest days of Machine Gun position development (1967-69) **Jimi Hendrix** pioneered the more advanced outro double knee-bend on haunches with extended major 10th fret-slide. This is a more difficult/ athletic approach, but the benefits are worth the effort. It is rumoured that the final three chords of **Van Halen**'s classic 1979 cover version of **The Kinks**' 'You Really Got Me' were recorded using this method, though guitarist **Edward Van Halen** has never confirmed this.

*Basic position:
12th fret sweep*

*Advanced position:
outro double knee-
bend on haunches with
extended major 10th
fret-slide position*

WARNING

DO NOT ATTEMPT THE OUTRO DOUBLE KNEE-BEND
ON HAUNCHES WITH EXTENDED MAJOR 10TH FRET-SLIDE
UNTIL YOU HAVE MASTERED THE BASIC POSITION.

TECHNIQUE:	*Tooth-picking (aka "playing with your teeth")*
AS USED BY:	*Buddy Guy, Jimi Hendrix, Iron Maiden*
REQUIREMENTS:	*Electric guitar, strap, teeth*
DIFFICULTY FACTOR:	*9/10 (Real) 3/10 (Fake)*
PREPOSTEROUSNESS RATING:	*7/10 (Both methods)*

There are two methods of dental picking – real and fake. The real (and altogether disappointing) method involves actually holding the guitar up to your face and plucking the strings with your teeth. On a Fender Stratocaster this is impossible due to the flat body and scratchplate. It is easier on curved guitars, including the Gibson ES-145 and Les Paul. Many players have attempted this but few have ever achieved musical results.

The correct method is to fake it. Hold the guitar up to your face, with the guitar body between your head and the audience. The picking hand holds the guitar with your fingers going round the side of the body, covering the strap button at the bridge end – this demonstrates to the audience that you don't have a hand free to pluck the notes. Then simply play hammer-ons and pull-offs using the fretting hand only. The audience can't see your face, so assume you're actually using your teeth.

HINT – it's very easy, as we all know, to play legato (hammer-on and pull-off licks) at great speed. Resist temptation here, and play slowly and deliberately – it makes the 'tooth-picked' notes sound more painful and difficult. If you can balance the guitar on your collar-bone and reach round with the picking hand to move the whammy bar, so much the better.

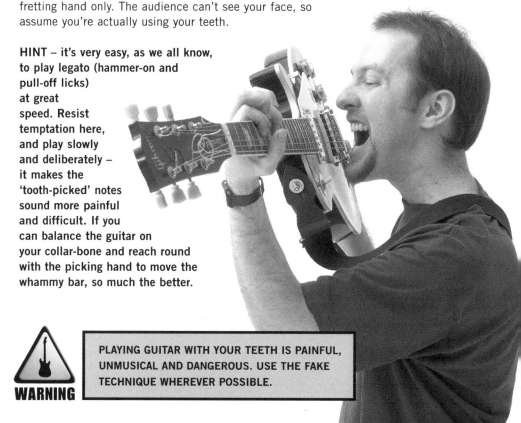

WARNING

PLAYING GUITAR WITH YOUR TEETH IS PAINFUL, UNMUSICAL AND DANGEROUS. USE THE FAKE TECHNIQUE WHEREVER POSSIBLE.

*Dental picking – real or fake?
Jimi took the secret to his grave.*

TECHNIQUE: *Twin-handed embracement picking*

REQUIREMENTS: *Guitar, strap, friend*

DIFFICULTY FACTOR: 4/10 **PREPOSTEROUSNESS RATING:** 7/10

As we learned from **T-bone Walker**'s 'behind the head' techniques, as long as your hands remain in the same position relative to the guitar and there aren't difficult position changes, you don't need to see the fingerboard. Twin-handed embracement picking works in the same way. The front guitarist plays the guitar normally, and the back one approaches from behind and reaches round the other player's waist to play the instrument.

The hands can be introduced both together, enabling the front player to grab tambourine or mic stand, or to clap their hands. Alternatively, you can try introducing them one at a time, so for a time both players are playing the instrument together. This is only really effective with very basic rhythm parts, because picking/timing accuracy is too difficult to co-ordinate easily. The technique was first popularised by the stage show *Return to the Forbidden Planet* in 1989, where it was performed using slap bass. **Hint – This is more impressive if the front player is taller.**

Twin-handed embracement picking – the front player here is performing a stylish mime.

Single-handed embracement picking may look good, as shown here, but it limits both players' musical options.

TECHNIQUE:	*Bidextral picking*
REQUIREMENTS:	*Two guitars, two straps, friend*
DIFFICULTY FACTOR: 6/10	PREPOSTEROUSNESS RATING: 7/10

For this unusual method, both players should stand facing each other.
The fingerboard hand should be fretting chords in the normal way. The picking/strumming hand reaches across to the opposite player's guitar and plays it in the normal way, but at arm's length.

To play rhythm guitar parts this way, ensure that the other player is fretting six string chords or at least muting unwanted open strings. Strumming accuracy is essential at this range. The technique doesn't work well for solos because of the synchronisation needed between players, but fingerstyle parts can be amazing when played in this way. It is rumoured that two Nashville session players created a version of 'Duelling Banjos' on guitar and banjo using this technique in 1987, but no recording exists. Sources close to the Nashville scene have suggested that this is merely urban folklore and such a thing would be impossible due to alternate tunings, differing number of strings, and objections from the US musicians' union.

Hint – Both guitarists should stand side-on to the audience, and as far away from each other as possible. Particularly effective when both players stand on a drum riser.

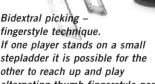

Bidextral picking – rhythm technique. Note that the plectrum hand has to face outward, requiring elbow rather than wrist pivot.

Bidextral picking – fingerstyle technique. If one player stands on a small stepladder it is possible for the other to reach up and play alternating thumb fingerstyle parts backwards, creating syncopations that cannot be achieved using any other method.

TECHNIQUE: *String percussion*

AS USED BY: *Grateful Dead, Tony Levin*

REQUIREMENTS: *Guitar, chair, drummer, sticks*

DIFFICULTY FACTOR: 9/10 | **PREPOSTEROUSNESS RATING:** 5/10

The guitarist sits in a chair, while the drummer lies on the floor, looking up towards the fingerboard, with the sticks across the strings. Alternatively, the guitarist stands while the drummer kneels in front of the guitar body. The easiest technique is simply to use open chord shapes, and let the drumsticks make contact 'flat' so they catch all the strings at once.

More complex 'dulcimer' effects can be achieved by working out arrangements where the drumsticks hit individual strings. This is more effective on acoustic guitar. The first recorded use of the technique was in 1967, by the **Grateful Dead** in their track 'The Golden Road (To Unlimited Devotion)'. In 1986, session bassist **Tony Levin** asked drummer **Jerry Marotta** to drum on his bass strings for the **Peter Gabriel** song *Big Time*. He went on to develop and manufacture 'funk fingers' – rubberised drumsticks that are worn by the bass player on the finger of the picking hand.

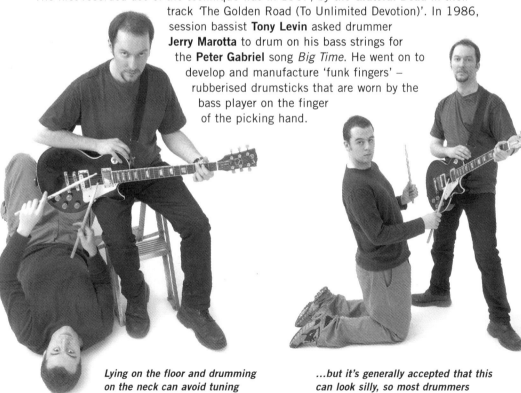

Lying on the floor and drumming on the neck can avoid tuning problems and pickup noise...

...but it's generally accepted that this can look silly, so most drummers prefer to kneel, like this.

WARNING

THE DRUMMER MUST AVOID HITTING THE STRINGS TOO HARD OR THEY MAY MAKE CONTACT WITH THE POLEPIECES OF THE PICKUP. THE GUITARIST SHOULD MUTE ANY UNWANTED OPEN STRINGS WITH THE (UNUSED) PICKING HAND.

TECHNIQUE: *Dodecaphonic guitar*

REQUIREMENTS: *Guitar & eleven other guitarists*

DIFFICULTY FACTOR: $^{10}/_{10}$ | **PREPOSTEROUSNESS RATING:** $^{9}/_{10}$

We've already seen how we you can have two guitarists playing the same guitar (see page 19), covering picking and fretting hands respectively. In the solo dodectet, this number is extended to twelve, simply by allocating two players to each string – one to pick, and one to fret.

The technique works best when using the entire range of the guitar, allowing for solo arrangements that cover up to three octaves. Picking hand players pluck one string each by reaching over the guitar body (using the first finger without a plectrum).

Fretting hand players cover a note each, and play by sliding their finger up or down by the minimum number of frets. The technique is only possible when the piece has been written specifically for a solo guitar dodectet. It is generally thought to be impossible to jam the blues on one guitar using twelve people.

Basic dodectet position – the example chord being played is A major 7th. An alternative dodectet position is the F minor 9th chord.

WARNING

IT IS RECOMMENDED THAT POTENTIAL DODECTET MEMBERS UNDERGO PHYSICAL TRAINING BEFORE ATTEMPTING THIS TECHNIQUE.

TASTELESS TECHNIQUES

Many musicians believe that thoughtful phrasing, correct rhythms, appropriate note choices and a pleasing tone are all you need to create a good guitar part. This is, of course, completely untrue. Where would guitar music be without the whammy bar, the capo, the, er, violin bow?

In this section we're going to look at some of the many playing techniques that players have used over the years (well, mostly the 1980s) to extend the sound of the guitar.

By following in the footsteps of these renowned innovators, you can learn to gargle, slither, dive-bomb, harp and pinch your way to success.

Some players consider it a compliment to be called 'tasteful'. But remember – those are all people who *can't play very fast*.

THE WHAMMY BAR

The whammy bar was originally called the 'vibrato bar' by inventor **Paul Bigsby**, and dubbed 'tremolo arm' by **Leo Fender** in the 1950s. The original idea was that all or part of the guitar's bridge would move slightly, creating subtle changes of pitch as the player wobbled the bar. Needless to say, guitar players weren't happy with the elegant sound of mere vibrato for very long. As early as 1959, **Hank Marvin** was using the bar for whole-tone bends (while dancing in a square – see page 48). By 1970, **Ritchie Blackmore** had started creating huge swoops (later known as dive-bombing) with the bar.

Then in 1978 American inventor **Floyd Rose** came up with a locking tremolo system. Because the strings were locked down at the nut and bridge, guitarists could pull and push the bar as much as they liked without going out of tune. The inevitable crash in the electronic guitar tuner market (23rd May 1979 – known as 'Dissonant Wednesday') – put many tuner designers out of work, some of whom found alternative employment in the digital watch industry. Throughout the 1980s everyone wore digital watches, until **Nirvana**'s *Nevermind* album featured **Kurt Cobain** playing a non-Floyd Rose guitar. The guitar's tuning was less stable, the tuner market picked up, and the designers went back to work.

Deep Purple's Ritchie Blackmore, shown here in the 1970s, shortly before the great guitar tuner industry collapse of 1979.

TECHNIQUE:	*Whammy bar vibrato*	
DIFFICULTY FACTOR:	2/10 (Normal)	5/10 (Whinny)
TASTELESS RATING:	1/10 (Normal)	9/10 (Whinny)

Pluck a note, let it ring on and then grab the bar with your picking hand. Wobble the bar very slightly after the note has been sounding for a moment. The most musical effect is achieved by pulling the bar up slightly as well as pressing it in, so that the vib goes above and below the original note's pitch. You can vib by just pressing and releasing the little finger on the bar, but this doesn't give you the up/down option. Some players use their little finger to create down-only vibrato.

A variation on vib is the 'whinny' – wobble the bar while dive-bombing downward (see page 31).

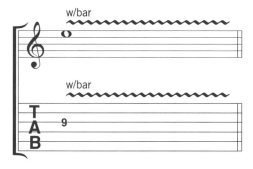

WARNING

BECAUSE WHAMMY BAR VIB IS SO MUCH EASIER THAN FINGER VIB, IT'S TEMPTING TO OVERDO IT.

Try to keep your bar vibrato subtle.

TECHNIQUE: *Pre-bend*

DIFFICULTY FACTOR: 3/10 | **TASTELESS RATING:** 2/10

N.B. Unfortunately, pre-bends can be very tasteful if not approached with recklessness

Push the bar in towards the body, pluck the note, then release the bar slowly so the note comes up to the correct pitch (adding vib if you want to).

If you're one of the many players that finds it difficult to keep normal 'fingered' string bends in tune, this method can fool most people (as long as you're facing away from the audience).

The earliest example of the whammy-bar pre-bend was, of course, Hank B. Marvin in the 1960s. Almost all of the Shadows' recordings featured this technique, which was later refined even further by Jeff Beck.

Below are four examples of whammy bar pre-bends. Each of these is designed to be a whole-tone (i.e. two frets' worth), though you can use any musical interval your whammy bar system can cope with.

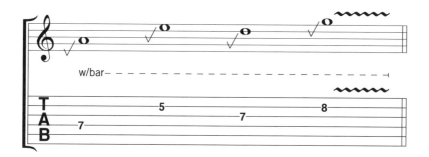

WARNING

IF YOU PRE-BEND TOO FAR ON A VINTAGE-STYLE STRAT TREMOLO
UNIT, THE STRINGS MAY STICK IN THE NUT AND GO SHARP IN PITCH,
ONLY SETTLING DOWN WHEN YOU DO A REGULAR FINGER-BEND.

TECHNIQUE: *Dips*

DIFFICULTY FACTOR: 2/10 | **TASTELESS RATING:** 6/10

N.B. Tasteless rating increases to 8/10 if you stick your tongue out!

Play a chord, let it ring on, then dip the bar in time with the music, letting the chord return to pitch each time. Easy.

Try combining pre-bends at the start of a lead guitar lick with dips while the notes ring on for some bizarre whale-like effects.

Dips can be rhythmically subtle if you're not careful. To avoid this, try combining them with other techniques – gargling, reverse dives or pinched harmonics. If this still creates a tasteful sound, you may have to save face by pretending that the dip was merely a precursor to a shake (see next page).

Here's an example of whammy bar dips – a power chord of A5, followed by three rhythmic dips.

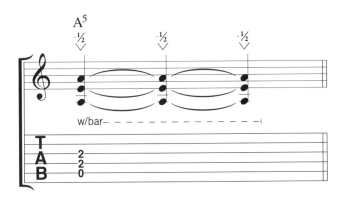

WARNING — WHEN YOU RELEASE THE DIP, DON'T LET THE BAR TWANG BACK TOO RAPIDLY OR YOU'LL CREATE AN UNINTENTIONAL GARGLE (SEE PAGE 32).

TECHNIQUE: Shakes

DIFFICULTY FACTOR: 3/10   **TASTELESS RATING:** 9/10

Exactly as vib, only more so. Play a note or chord, then shake the bar up and down violently. Play hammer-ons and pull-offs with the fingerboard hand while your picking hand is otherwise engaged with the whammy bar.

The technique sounds at its maddest when the amp is set so loud/distorted that feedback harmonics are created. Alternatively, play pinched or open harmonics while shaking the bar.

WARNING

NO WARNINGS HERE. THE TECHNIQUE SOUNDS STUPID. JUST GO WITH IT.

If you can build up an emotional frenzy while shaking the bar as shown here, the vibrato will generally be wider.

TECHNIQUE: *Motorbikin' (aka Motorcyclin')*

DIFFICULTY FACTOR: 4/10 | **TASTELESS RATING:** 8/10

Dip and hold the bar as for a reverse dive. Then pluck the bass E string and raise the bar a little over a period of around two seconds (did I mention that nearly all whammy bar effects sound better with distortion?). Next, quickly dip the bar slightly from its current position to create a 'gear change', and begin raising it slowly again. Repeat the procedure up to five times, and if necessary start pulling the bar upward from its rest position.

The illusion is of a motorbike revving through the gears. Try it on the A string for a 50cc moped, and the D string for a lawnmower.

NOTE – very few lawnmowers have 5 gears, so for authenticity try to restrict yourself to no more than three dips of the bar as you ascend. The Honda H2113SDA Lawn Tractor is a notable 5-speed exception, but its tone is very difficult to emulate without a germanium diode fuzzbox.

The acceleration of the Honda H2113SDA Lawn Tractor can be emulated by using a series of five equally-spaced reverse dives and dips on the D string.

WARNING

BECAUSE THIS TECHNIQUE IS, EFFECTIVELY, A COMPLICATED REVERSE DIVE, THE NOTE CAN DIE OUT EASILY. SET THE AMP LOUD AND STAND NEXT TO IT. THIS WILL HELP TO DRIVE THE STRING AND IF YOU'RE LUCKY, CAN TRIGGER A HARMONIC.

The legendary Steve Vai – the best whammy user, bar none.

TECHNIQUE: *Dive-bombing*

DIFFICULTY FACTOR: *1/10 (Regular) 3/10 (Harmonics)*

TASTELESS RATING: *7/10 (Both methods)*

To play a regular dive, play a note, then push the
bar in toward the guitar body so the note goes down rapidly in pitch. With most
whammy bar units (the only exception being Steinberger's famous 'Trans-trem')
this is more effective on the bass strings, when the dive can be an octave or more.
The thinner strings – the top E particularly – will only let you dive a few frets' worth.

There are three main variations – **harmonic dive**, **reverse dive** and **motorbikin'**
(see page 29). To play a harmonic dive, pluck any open harmonic (my personal
favourite is the fourth fret on the 'G' string) and depress the bar as normal.
At high volumes this note can really 'squeal'.

A reverse dive is a grandiose version of a pre-bend. Press the bar as far as it will
go without the strings hitting the pickup, then pluck the string. You will then need
to raise the bar *quickly* to avoid the flapping string losing energy and turning your
ascending dive-bomber into a malfunctioning hairdryer.

WARNING

IF YOU PUSH THE BAR TOO FAR DOWN, THE STRINGS MAY LOSE SO
MUCH TENSION THAT THEY TOUCH THE POLEPIECES ON THE GUITAR'S
MAGNETIC PICKUPS. THIS RESULTS IN AN UNPLEASANT 'CLUNK' AND
THE ABRUPT END OF THE NOTE.

TECHNIQUE: *Gargling (aka 'flicks')*

DIFFICULTY FACTOR: *5/10* | **TASTELESS RATING:** *6/10*

Pluck a note, then push the bar, letting your finger slide off the end immediately afterwards so the unit 'boings' back into place. The resulting vibration gives a harsh mechanical-sounding vibrato that is impossible to achieve any other way.

The most common method is to hold the bar in the normal playing position and flick your finger down towards the pickups. However, some players prefer to reverse the bar so it's facing away from the bridge, and flick the finger back towards the body.

The usual position for gargling results in a gargle that begins with a very slight lowering in pitch. The reverse position begins with a slight rise in pitch before the gargle.

Gargling works best if the whammy bar is firmly fixed in position rather than swinging loose. On a Strat-type bridge unit this can be achieved by rotating the bar until it is tight in the socket, floating parallel to the strings.

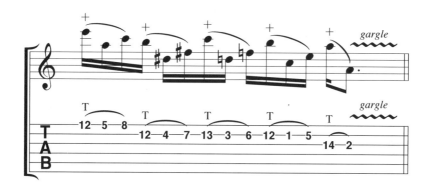

WARNING

YOU NEED A TRULY FLOATING BRIDGE SETUP FOR THIS TO WORK. IF THE BRIDGE IS FLAT TO THE BODY WHEN AT REST (AS ON SOME FENDER STRATS) YOU NEED TO ADD MORE SPRINGS INTO THE BACK OF THE UNIT UNTIL THE BAR CAN BE PULLED UP AS WELL AS PRESSED DOWN.

Nuno Bettencourt's use of gargling in the early 1990s was always Extreme...

TECHNIQUE: *Ebow*

DIFFICULTY FACTOR: 6/10 **TASTELESS RATING:** 2/10

The Ebow rests on two of the guitar's non-adjacent strings (e.g. the first and third) and electronically 'drives' the middle one without the player plucking the string. It creates a smooth, constant tone with lots of harmonics. Because it's most effective when played on a single string, players usually adapt their technique (or songs) to ensure the melody moves up and down, rather than across the fingerboard.

You'll have heard the Ebow on recordings by dozens of bands including **Big Country**, **Blondie**, **the Cranberries**, **U2**, **Metallica**, **Oasis**, and **REM** (the 1996 track 'Ebow The Letter').

WARNING

THE EBOW TAKES A LOT OF GETTING USED TO BECAUSE IT MEANS PLAYING THE GUITAR IN A COMPLETELY DIFFERENT WAY. BE PREPARED FOR A LONG PERIOD OF ADJUSTMENT. AND IT WON'T LET YOU PLAY BOX SHAPE PENTATONIC BLUES LICKS. HURRAH!

TECHNIQUE: *Violining*

DIFFICULTY FACTOR: 5/10   TASTELESS RATING: 3/10

Turn the guitar's volume down, pluck the note, then immediately turn up the volume again using the little finger of the picking hand. The 'twang' of the note's attack disappears, and you're left with a smoother sound reminiscent of a violin – especially if you're using distortion.

Develop a technique that involves upward-picking the note then rolling the volume control up with the little finger as one movement, then turning the volume control down again just before you pick the next note. If you take care to mute unwanted open strings with the fingerboard hand, it is possible to play violining licks very quickly, further disguising the guitar's sound. If you can manage whammy bar vib as well, you can achieve 'cello-like effects on the bass strings.

Some players choose to use a volume pedal instead of the guitar's volume control (e.g. **George Harrison**'s chords on the **Beatles**' 'I Need You'). There are also slow-attack noise gates available on most guitar multi-FX that will enable auto-violining.

To achieve violining using the guitar's volume control, you'll need to stretch the little finger out like this.

WARNING

THIS IS VERY DIFFICULT ON SOME GIBSON GUITARS DUE TO THE POSITION OF THE VOLUME CONTROL IN RELATION TO THE PICKING POSITION. IF YOU WANT TO ACHIEVE VIOLINING SOUNDS ON A LES PAUL, FOR INSTANCE, TRY A VOLUME PEDAL.

TECHNIQUE: *Pickup switching*

DIFFICULTY FACTOR: 2/10   **TASTELESS RATING:** 2/10

Switch off one pickup by turning its volume control down to zero. Turn the other pickup to full volume. Now play a chord and move the switch in time with the music while it rings out – you'll get a rhythmic on-off effect.

The technique was pioneered by **Pete Townshend** on **The Who**'s *Can't Explain*, and later used by **Hendrix** (moving the Strat's selector switch for a more subtle tonal version of the effect due to the fact that you can't turn individual Strat pickups off).

More recently, the technique appeared on the **Pearl Jam** song 'Garden' (played by PJ guitarist **Mike McReady**). **Peter Buck** (**REM**) and **Johnny Marr** (**The Smiths**) have used square-wave tremolo effects to create automatic on-off versions of the same sound.

Make sure one pickup is turned down to zero, then use the selector switch as shown to turn the chord on and off.

WARNING THIS IS JUST ABOUT POSSIBLE ON A STRAT, BUT MUCH MORE EFFECTIVE ON A GUITAR THAT HAS SEPARATE VOLUME CONTROLS FOR EACH PICKUP (E.G. GIBSON 335 OR LES PAUL).

As Mike McCready knows well, the Flying V's selector switch layout makes it ideal for pickup switching techniques.

TECHNIQUE: *Pick scrape*

DIFFICULTY FACTOR: 3/10

TASTELESS RATING: 7/10

Set up a loud, fairly distorted guitar sound, and then touch the edge of the plectrum to one or two of the wound bass strings of the guitar. Then simply scrape the pick along the strings. If you can time it right, the scrape should end on a first-position power chord (e.g. open A5) – the technique here is to pluck with the plectrum exactly on the bar-line as you get to the end of the slide.

The problem, of course, is making this aggressive-sounding technique look good on stage when you're only moving your hand very slowly.

Jumping off the drum riser while doing scissor-kicks is one option (painful/risky, but worked for **Paul Weller** in the early days of **The Jam**).

Pick scrapes are pretty tasteless really. Almost as much of a rock cliché as jumping up and down on the last three chords.

WARNING

THE PICK SCRAPE IS ALL ABOUT... TIMING. MAKE SURE YOUR SCRAPE ENDS ON THE BARLINE. SCRAPE TOO FAST AND IT SOUNDS LIKE YOU'VE MADE A MISTAKE.

TECHNIQUE: *Nut bend*

DIFFICULTY FACTOR: $6/10$ **TASTELESS RATING:** $1/10$

Play an open string as normal, then press the string back against the headstock, behind the nut (see photo). You tighten the string temporarily and this raises its pitch. The effect is similar to a lap steel. As well as the basic nut bend up, there are three main variations. A *nut pre-bend* involves pressing the string into the headstock before you pluck it, then releasing it. A *double nut bend* (see TAB) uses a different finger on two or more strings. Nut vibrato involves quickly pressing and releasing the string behind the nut. Some players find nut vibrato easier to control than finger vibrato.

Obviously the technique only works when there is sufficient depth behind the nut to achieve a good-sized bend – this is why most people find it easier on a Telecaster. The undisputed king of the nut bend is country guitarist **Jerry Donahue**.

A single nut-bend. Blisters go with the territory.

This double nut bend is more difficult – you also need to make sure you're not touching the open third string while you bend the other two.

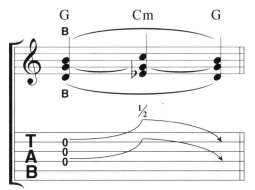

 WARNING

GO ANY HIGHER THAN .010 GAUGE STRINGS, AND THIS IS GOING TO *HURT*.

Pluck the D, G and B strings with the picking hand, then play the double nut bend to raise the pitch of the D and B by one semitone each, then release. You should hear chord changes of G-Cm-G.

Pete Townshend – the inventor, and still the undisputed king, of the quadruple windmill.

TECHNIQUE: *Windmill*

DIFFICULTY FACTOR: 3/10   **TASTELESS RATING:** 8/10

The standard windmill, like playing with teeth, is mainly an illusion. The audience gets the impression that you're attacking the guitar with such force that your hand needs a spin-bowler style run-up to achieve that power chord. Actually the chord strum is a fairly gentle upstroke, but it's preceded by such a dramatic swing of the arm that everyone is fooled.

A variation on the technique shown here is the triple (or even quadruple) windmill, where the arm rotates several times, gradually speeding up, until making contact with the strings on the final upstroke.

1. Triple anti-clockwise windmill – starting position...

2. Descend, rotating the arm so it's moving anti-clockwise from the audience's point of view.

3. Ascend again, and repeat as many times as necessary until you're ready to play the chord...

4. Finally, catch all the strings in an upstroke, muting any that you don't want with the fingerboard hand.

WARNING

ALWAYS START THE WINDMILL MOTION IN AN UPWARD DIRECTION. A DOWNWARD WINDMILL IS MORE LIKELY TO BRING YOUR KNUCKLES INTO CONTACT WITH THE EDGE OF THE FINGERBOARD AND THEREAFTER INTO CONTACT WITH A PLASTER CAST.

TECHNIQUE: *Two-handed playing (aka tapping, widdling)*

DIFFICULTY FACTOR: 6/10-10/10   **TASTELESS RATING:** 9/10

The idea is simple – use the picking hand's finger (usually the second finger) to fret a note by tapping onto the fret, then pull off from that position to a lower note – either an open string, or more often another note fretted by the fingerboard hand. The advantage of the technique is that it's relatively easy to do this very rapidly indeed.

Add combinations of normal hammer-ons and pull-offs, and you can create complex-sounding arpeggios on a single string.

After **Eddie Van Halen**'s pioneering instrumental track 'Eruption' in 1978, a decade's worth of two-handed players emerged (by which I mean that they used tapping techniques – players with two hands have generally been the norm in guitar playing circles for centuries).

On the page opposite you'll find a selection of tapping licks that cover most of the basics of the technique.

Although it's hard to improve on a tasteless rating of 9/10, you can do so by using an '80s Steinberger headless 6-string (as shown).

WARNING

IF YOU ARE GOING TO GET INTO TAPPING, YOU MUST ENSURE YOU ARE ABLE TO MUTE ALL THE UNWANTED OPEN STRINGS. IF ANY EXTRA NOTES RING OUT, THE CLARITY OF THE NOTES WILL BE LOST – THIS PROBLEM WILL BE EXACERBATED BY HEAVY DISTORTION.

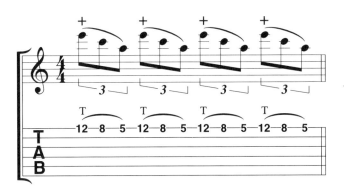

A standard descending triplet – the picking hand taps at the 12th fret, pulls off to the 8th, then the fingerboard hand pulls off from the 8th to the 5th, then the whole pattern repeats. This is the one everyone learns first. Use it on stage at your peril.

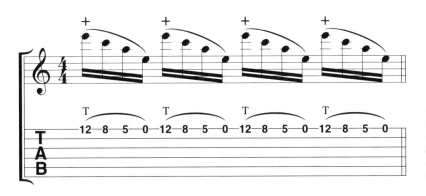

Use two fingerboard hand pull-offs and you can get a pattern of four descending notes.

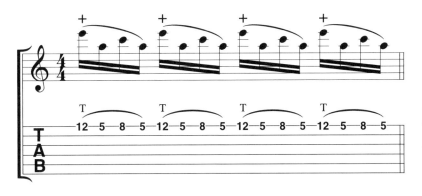

This group of four notes uses hammer-ons and pull-offs from the fingerboard hand, and is fairly easy to play at an upsetting speed.

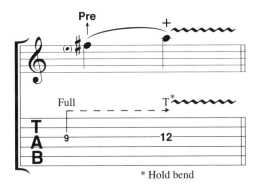

* Hold bend

A single high tap with vib. Note that the tap arrives when the string is already bent up a whole tone by the fingerboard hand, which adds the vibrato while the fretting hand simply holds the note.

TECHNIQUE: *Amp feedback*

DIFFICULTY FACTOR: 2/10 | TASTELESS RATING: 1/10

Set up a distorted amp tone, and turn it up loud. Then pick any note very gently, and move towards the amp. The string should feed back – i.e. the note should ring on indefinitely without you having to pick the note again. If it doesn't work straight away, try turning up the amp or picking the note slightly harder.

The note may also gradually evolve into a harmonic (see page 46), especially if you add gentle vibrato.

This is musical feedback – i.e. you, the player, are in control of the notes. It should not be confused with pickup feedback, an unpleasant high-pitched squealing created by playing with cheap pickups through a loud amp.

NOTE – If it doesn't work straight away, either turn up the amp, or hold the end of the headstock against the edge of the cabinet – the vibrations are transmitted through the guitar's body.

Fret any note and stand next to the amp. Make sure it's turned up loud.

TECHNIQUE: *Banjo roll (aka fingerstyle cross-picking)*

DIFFICULTY FACTOR: 9/10 **TASTELESS RATING:** 3/10

If your fingerboard hand can manage the stretches, it's possible to play three notes that are adjacent in a musical scale on three different strings. Because the picking hand's fingers can pluck notes in rapid succession on different strings, it follows that you can create faster scale runs by playing across the guitar's fingerboard rather than along it.

Banjo rolling works best if you use your thumb and first two fingers. The example in the TAB is a complete scale run, going across the fingerboard and ending on an F – the lick works well over a chord of G7. Marked underneath the notation is a letter name that shows which finger plucks each note ('p' means the thumb, 'i' the index finger and 'm' the middle finger). Banjo rolls are very difficult to play, and don't always suit distorted sounds, so they've been mainly used by country virtuosos such as **Chet Atkins**, **Brent Mason**, **Albert Lee** and **Jerry Donahue**.

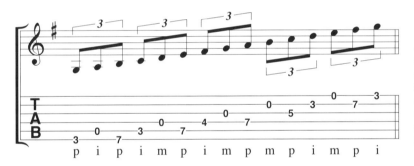

A scalic pattern using banjo rolls – note that the fingerboard hand needs to stretch to ensure that the open string rings out clearly.

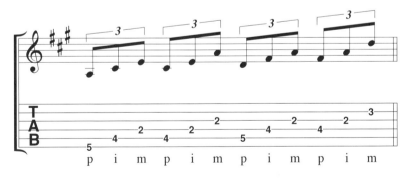

A banjo roll applied to an arpeggio. As before, the fingerboard hand should hold down all of the notes throughout the roll rather than trying to fret each one individually.

WARNING

IT IS PROFESSIONAL SUICIDE TO ADMIT TO BEING MUSICALLY INFLUENCED BY THE BANJO. ALWAYS REFER TO THIS TECHNIQUE AS FINGERSTYLE CROSS-PICKING WHEN IN THE PRESENCE OF MUSICIANS OR BANJO PLAYERS.

TECHNIQUE: *Harmonics*

DIFFICULTY FACTOR: *3/10 (Natural) to 9/10 (Tapped)*

TASTELESS RATING: *8/10 (All methods)*

The principle of a harmonic is this: if you stop a string from vibrating at certain points along its length, it will have no alternative but to vibrate in fractions of its length, creating a higher note. So if you stop an open string from vibrating exactly half-way along its length (by touching it just over the 12th fret before you pick) a note an octave higher – or 'first harmonic' will be created. The strongest harmonics occur 12, 7, 5 and 4 frets above the original note (or 'fundamental'). To ensure that the harmonic sounds clearly, you need to stop the string directly over the relevant fret rather than between frets as with normal playing.

Harmonics can create high-pitched notes that are a long way outside the normal range of the guitar; and they also have a different tone from normal picked notes. Interestingly, dogs can hear higher harmonics than humans. If you are beginning to notice that audiences are growing less interested in your music, but the gigs are attracting more chihuahuas and poodles than previously, it's almost certainly because of the development of upper harmonics in your solos.

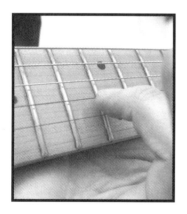

Natural harmonics.
Touch the string over the 12th fret, pluck the open note firmly, then immediately remove the fingerboard hand to let the harmonic ring out clearly.

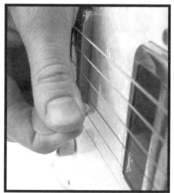

Pinched harmonics.
(sound best with distortion)
Dig into the string near the pickups with only a tiny bit of the edge of the plectrum, catching the string with the side of the picking hand's thumb as you remove your hand. This is how metal players add that 'squeal' to single notes.

Tapped harmonics.
Fret any note, then tap sharply onto the fingerboard over the node (usually 12 frets higher) with the picking hand, removing the hand as soon as you've made contact.

WARNING

PINCHED HARMONICS MAKE YOU SOUND LIKE YOU'RE A MUCH BETTER ROCK LEAD PLAYER THAN YOU ARE. OTHER GUITARISTS, HOWEVER, ARE ALSO AWARE OF THIS, AND WILL SEE THROUGH IT IN A SECOND.

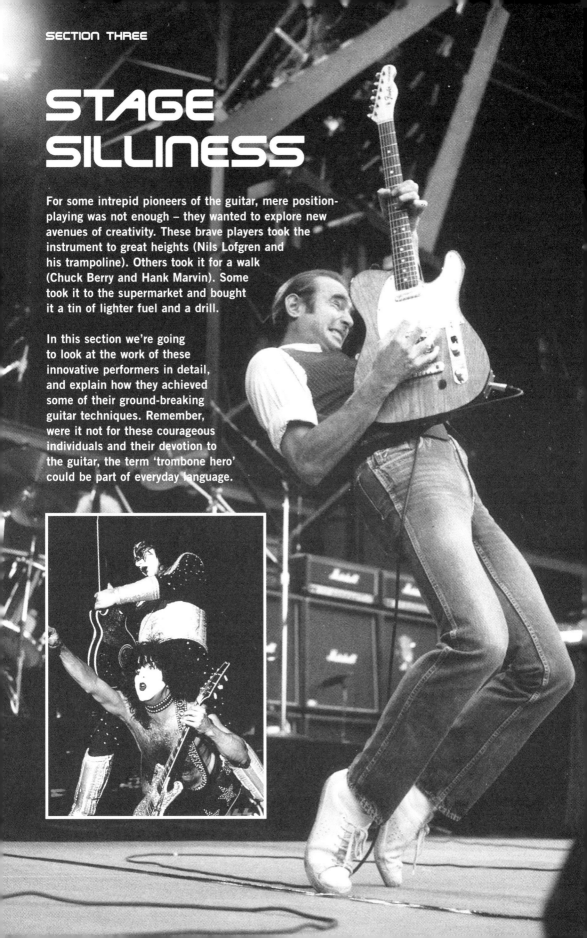

STAGE SILLINESS

For some intrepid pioneers of the guitar, mere position-playing was not enough – they wanted to explore new avenues of creativity. These brave players took the instrument to great heights (Nils Lofgren and his trampoline). Others took it for a walk (Chuck Berry and Hank Marvin). Some took it to the supermarket and bought it a tin of lighter fuel and a drill.

In this section we're going to look at the work of these innovative performers in detail, and explain how they achieved some of their ground-breaking guitar techniques. Remember, were it not for these courageous individuals and their devotion to the guitar, the term 'trombone hero' could be part of everyday language.

TECHNIQUE: *Walking in the Shadows*

REQUIREMENTS: *Fender Stratocaster with strap, feet*

DIFFICULTY FACTOR: 9/10 **SILLINESS RATING:** 9/10

"Left foot forward. Right foot crosses over to the left side of the left foot. Left foot diagonally back so that it is directly behind right foot. Right foot back to original position."

This mantra was chanted to **Hank B Marvin** by fellow Shadows **Bruce Welch** and **Jet Harris** in rehearsals throughout the late 1950s. By 1960 the band had developed the move into a fine art. **Hank** even managed to smile while executing the forward step, which is all the more remarkable when you take into account the challengingly high silliness rating of the technique. No-one has dared to imitate the footwork of those early shows – even **Hank** himself now omits it from his live shows.

There have been no confirmed cases of the Shadows walk resulting in injury. However, if you choose to experiment with the Shadows walk as shown here, neither Joe Bennett, Wise Publications nor any of their associates can be held legally responsible for any damages arising out of embarrassment this may cause.

1. Left foot forward...   *2. Right foot round to the other side...*

The Shadows were among the first exponents of the walk after which the group was named.

3. *Left foot diagonally back...*

4. *...and right foot back into position.*

TECHNIQUE: *Duck-walking*

REQUIREMENTS: *Gibson semi-solid guitar, sensible shoes*

DIFFICULTY FACTOR: 3/10   **SILLINESS RATING:** 5/10

Chuck Berry invented the technique in the mid-1950s, and continued to use it for the rest of his career. It is so heavily associated with him that any player who uses it is considered merely to be making a respectful reference to his influence on their playing.

The basic technique (for a right-handed player) involves bending the right leg, putting all the bodyweight on it, then stretching out the left leg at a 32 degree angle with the heel touching the ground. The left foot should protrude upward at a 90 degree angle. The player then hops (four crotchets per bar at around ♩=145) on the supporting leg, allowing the left foot to swing naturally up in the air. As the body descends, the supporting knee should bend slightly more to absorb the impact. At the same moment the heel of the protruding foot should come into contact with the floor and immediately bounce back into the air.

Although **Chuck** mainly used the technique to go forwards across the front of the stage, an experienced duck-walker should be able to use the technique to go backwards if necessary.

32°

WARNING SHOCK CAN BE TRANSMITTED UP THE LEG OF THE LEADING FOOT, AND MUSCLE CRAMP CAN DEVELOP EASILY IN THE SUPPORTING LEG. AND YOU COULD THROW YOUR BACK OUT.

Ever the innovator, Chuck Berry is shown here executing a standard duck-walk combined with an inverted machine-gun and soloing gurn-wince. The home key is B♭ major.

TECHNIQUE: *Back-to-back (aka limbo guitar)*

REQUIREMENTS: *Two guitars, two guitarists, two straps*

DIFFICULTY FACTOR: 4/10 | **SILLINESS RATING:** 8/10

The simplest form of the back-to-back
arrived in the early 1970s, and coincided unsurprisingly with the development of
harmonised twin-lead guitar solos as featured on recordings by **Wishbone Ash** and
Thin Lizzy. (Obviously **Queen**'s **Brian May** was the undisputed king of harmonised
solos at the time, but he avoided the technique in the band's live shows as it would
have necessitated standing back-to-back with an Echoplex tape machine.)

The most common method involves both players standing with synchronised
shoulder-blades, side-on to the audience. A less well-known and more challenging
variation is for each guitarist's head to rest on the shoulder of the other – see picture.

The advent of Techno in the early 1990s and the depersonalisation of socio-cultural
communication in rock during the middle of that decade led to a gradual
reduction in back-to-back techniques, but
it's still a worthwhile technique to study,
if only for its historical value.

WARNING

IF THE GAP BETWEEN PLAYERS IS
TOO GREAT IT CAN BE IMPOSSIBLE TO
SELF-RIGHT. IN THIS INSTANCE IT CAN BE
APPROPRIATE TO MOVE IMMEDIATELY
INTO A DOUBLE DYING FLY (SEE PAGE 54).

TECHNIQUE: *Disco pick-fling*

REQUIREMENTS: *Guitar, strap, fluorescent plectrum*

DIFFICULTY FACTOR: 7/10 | **SILLINESS RATING:** 8/10

Play a chord, then throw the plectrum up in the air while the chord rings out. As the plectrum reaches the apex of its flight, rotate your whole body (pivoting on one foot) through 360 degrees quickly. When you come to a standstill, reach up to grab the descending plectrum, and play another chord.

1. Throw the plectrum up in the air...

2... then spin around...

3... and catch it again.

WARNING

ENSURE THAT YOU ALWAYS USE A FLUORESCENT PLECTRUM WHEN EXECUTING AN ON-STAGE PICK-FLING, OR THE AUDIENCE WILL BE UNABLE TO SEE THE PICK, AND BE MYSTIFIED BY YOUR COMPLEX AND INEXPLICABLE SEQUENCE OF TWIRLING BODY MOVES.

TECHNIQUE: *The dying fly*

REQUIREMENTS: *Guitar, strap*

DIFFICULTY FACTOR: 3/10 | **SILLINESS RATING:** 10/10

Lie on your back while playing a solo. It sounds simple, and indeed the technique is not challenging for most experienced players. The difficulty is not in doing the Dying Fly itself, but in getting back on your feet again.

Many players have pondered over how to achieve post-DF equilibrium. The only success that has been documented (or, if you will, rockumented) is credited to **Nigel Tufnel**, guitarist with the legendary metal band **Spinal Tap**. After the band's reconciliation during the historic *Smell The Glove* tour, he attempted a brave *single*-limbo position, and developed this into an impromptu Dying Fly.
His answer was simply to call a roadie to get him into an upright playing position. Not a note of the solo was missed. Genius.

WARNING IT IS POSSIBLE TO DO AN INADVERTENT DYING FLY BY TAKING A BACK-TO-BACK DOUBLE-LIMBO TOO FAR.

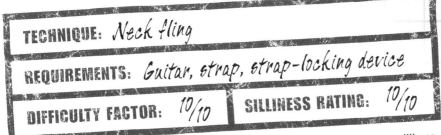

TECHNIQUE: *Neck fling*

REQUIREMENTS: *Guitar, strap, strap-locking device*

DIFFICULTY FACTOR: *10/10*   SILLINESS RATING: *10/10*

NB. This is the 'holy grail' of on-stage silliness.

The guitar is spun around the player's head, using the neck (of the player, not the guitar) as a pivot. The momentum of the initial 'throw' of the guitar carries it round behind the player, who moves their neck to swing it further around. Eventually the guitar returns to the playing position.

If the initial throw is not hard enough, the guitar will stall mid-flight and fall without achieving the full rotation. If it is too hard the resulting centrifugal force may cause the player to be thrown off-balance and fall without achieving the full rotation.

The neck-fling has been used most recently by **Paul Draper** (**Mansun**) and **Cone** (**Sum 41**).

Throw the guitar up and behind you...

...and let the strap pivot on your neck as it swings back to the playing position.

THIS IS HIGHLY DANGEROUS IN A CONFINED SPACE. WHILE THIS BOOK WAS BEING WRITTEN, THREE RESEARCHERS, A PHOTOGRAPHER AND A LAMPSTAND WERE SLIGHTLY DAMAGED.

WARNING

GUITAR ABUSE

So far, we've only concerned ourselves with the player's contribution to extreme techniques. Now we are going to look at the guitar itself and how it is possible to challenge the tyrannical mediocrity of the finger, plectrum and bottleneck that has kept guitar players musically imprisoned all these years.

Feel free to develop the ideas shown in this section using your own household objects. Cornflakes or rice in the soundhole of a Martin D12 (or any large-bodied American flat-topped acoustic) can create complex polyrhythms if the player jumps up and down while strumming semiquavers. Hitting Rickenbacker pickups with salad tongs or dessert cutlery will add a pleasing metallic sound that to this day is very rarely heard in live performance. And, of course, sandpaper tied to a toddler's hands or cat's tail can make a useful abrasive sound, rich in third harmonics, when your child or pet brushes against the guitar's strings.

ACCESSORY: *Violin bow*

AS USED BY: *Jimmy Page*

The guitar is simply bowed in the normal way, like a violin or 'cello.

Because the radius of the guitar's fingerboard is almost flat compared to orchestral stringed instruments, the technique really only works on the outer two strings.

HINTS AND TIPS

USE AN ARCHTOP GUITAR (E.G. LES PAUL) IF AT ALL POSSIBLE – THE FLAT BODY OF A STRAT MAKES BOWING ALMOST IMPOSSIBLE.

ACCESSORY: *Drill*

AS USED BY: *Mr Big (Billy Sheehan and Paul Gilbert)*

A rotating plectrum (or rather, a plectrum – the drill supplies the rotation) is fixed to the end of the drill as shown.

The drill (a *Makita* cordless model) is then moved closer to the strings until the edge of the plectrum makes contact.

The resulting tremolando picking is faster than a human hand can manage.

HINTS AND TIPS

USE A MEDIUM-LIGHT PLECTRUM.
AND A CORDLESS DRILL.

ACCESSORY: *Cigarette Lighter*

AS USED BY: *Early bluesmen, Jimi Hendrix*

There are two guitar techniques centring around the cigarette lighter. The first is to use a metal 'Zippo' style lighter as a bottleneck (see pint glass, page 60).

The second is, of course, to use lighter fluid to set fire to your guitar, as famously pioneered by **Jimi Hendrix**.

HINTS AND TIPS

MOST EXPERIENCED GUITAR TEACHERS WILL ADVISE YOU TO BE VERY CAREFUL WHENEVER YOU SET FIRE TO YOUR GUITAR. IT IS ADVISABLE ON A STRAT-TYPE GUITAR TO SPREAD THE LIGHTER FUEL AROUND THE BODY RATHER THAN THE SCRATCHPLATE AREA. IF IN ANY DOUBT AT ALL, USE THE SAFER (BUT LESS VISUALLY IMPRESSIVE) OPTION OF BARBECUE GEL.

ACCESSORY: *Beer glass*

AS USED BY: *Ry Cooder*

Put the guitar into an open tuning, and use the beer glass as a huge bottleneck. The easiest way to do this is to push your whole hand inside a pint glass and play with it upside down. A more impressive technique is to play with the glass half full (or half empty). Beware of getting your hand stuck in the glass.

HINTS AND TIPS

BECAUSE OF THE WIDE RADIUS OF A GLASS COMPARED TO A BOTTLENECK, IT IS MORE DIFFICULT TO PITCH NOTES ACCURATELY. WITH THIS IN MIND, PLAY WIDE, IMPRESSIVE SWOOPS UP TO THE CHORD RATHER THAN SUBTLY TASTEFUL BLUES LICKS.

ACCESSORY: *Microphone stand*

AS USED BY: *Alvin Lee, Jimmy Page, Pete Townshend*

A microphone stand can make an excellent bottleneck. The technique is the same as regular slide, except that the guitar moves instead of the bottleneck.

This is more difficult than it sounds, and prolonged use should be avoided, but for the occasional sliding chord along the fingerboard, it's hard to beat.

HINTS AND TIPS

STRAIGHT CHROME STANDS ARE EASIER TO USE THAN BOOM STANDS. TRY IT AND YOU'LL SEE WHAT I MEAN.

OUTRO

So now you've got everything you need to know to push your guitar playing to its *real* limits. But to achieve the ultimate performance on stage, you need to add that vital ingredient – sincerity.

Shown here are a selection of classic facial expressions that guitarists use to simulate concentration and emotional involvement when they're playing. If you can master even a few of these you will be sure to be respected as a serious guitar player. And if you can create an expression more extreme than anything you see here, you will be well on your way to being a true guitar innovator.

IT'S EASY TO BLUFF...

Be an instant success with *It's Easy To Bluff*. Short biographies of top players, a history of the style, specialist guitar techniques and all the skills and secrets you'll need to know to pass yourself off as a bluffer-par-excellence!

Blues Guitar AM955196
Acoustic Guitar AM955174

Rock Guitar AM955218
Metal Guitar AM955207

Jazz Guitar AM955185
Music Theory AM958485

REALLY EASY GUITAR!

Each of the books in the *Really Easy Guitar!* series contains songs arranged in the easy to-follow 'chords and lyrics' style, with full 'soundalike' backing tracks to play along to. There are also hints and tips for each song, and excerpts of TAB for the famous riffs or intros that you've always wanted to learn. Everything you need to know to play your favourite songs!

The Beatles NO90692
Rock Classics AM957693

21st Century Rock AM975645
Nü Metal AM976283

Bryan Adams AM971806
90s Hits AM957715

JOE BENNETT is a guitar teacher, sessionist and lecturer in Commercial Music at Bath Spa University College. Joe's other publications include the *Guitar...To Go!* and *It's Easy To Bluff* series, and he is a regular contributor to *Total Guitar*, *Future Music* and *Music Tech* magazines.